Sworn To Secrecy

Sworn To Secrecy

Poetry written by me and interpreted by you

Ursula Lumpkin

Copyright © 2018 LeUrsula Lumpkin

All rights reserved. No part of this may be used or reproduced in any manner whatsoever without written permission except in the case of brief quotations embodied in critical articles and reviews. Printed in the United States of America.

Green Sea Publishing, LLC

ISBN-13: 978-0692188248

ISBN-10: 069218824X

ATTENTION: SCHOOLS AND BUSINESSES

Green Sea Publishing, LLC books are available at quantity discounts with bulk purchase for educational, business, or sales promotional use. For information, please email lumpkin_11@yahoo.com

Instagram, Twitter: @ursulalumpkin

#SwornToSecrecy

Sworn To Secrecy

I dedicate this book to you, mom. Thanks for never making me feel alone in this world and encouraging my ideas, even when you didn't fully understand. I can still hear your voice in my ear, "You can do anything you want, you only fail when you stop trying." I hope I'm doing you justice. Keep watching over me. I miss you.

Sworn To Secrecy

We live in a world where people want you to think for yourself but not too much, or in a way that may hinder them. My concept behind interpreting for yourself, is I don't want to tell you how to see things. We all see and hear things differently. What one may interpret as love, another may interpret as hate. So, pull up a chair or sit on the floor. Grab your favorite writing pen/pencil. Tuck yourself into your favorite cubby hole or lock yourself inside your man cave. Wherever you choose, let your imagination run wild. Enjoy.

Ursula Lumpkin

Sworn To Secrecy

THESE POEMS INTERPRETED BY:

_____

Sworn To Secrecy

Title: _____

Pick a color from the rainbow, and I'll fetch it for you.

Command your second wish, and I'll grant it for you.

Spat out lyrics from your favorite song, and I'll play it for you.

Tell me you want to read by moonlight, and I'll throw a lasso around the moon and pull it near you.

Name the one who wronged you, and I'll slay the dragon for you.

Pluck a flower from a garden, and I'll watch it wither away with you.

Declare anything and I'll make a way for you.

-Ursula Lumpkin

Sworn To Secrecy
Title: _____

I'm shook.

It's the way your hair moves when the wind blows, like that gust was only for you.

You're kissed by sunrays, can I always live this day?

Whisper in my ear, so no matter the chatter, it's your voice I hear.

Like the nights before Christmas, is this one for me?

If I were to speak aloud your beauty, sunflowers would grow green with envy.

-Ursula Lumpkin

Sworn To Secrecy

Title: _____

Stare down the sun, rather than see her smile at someone new.

She knew.

Overprotection becomes jealousy.

She knew that too.

I'm losing my bearings,

Becoming unglued.

My spirits in shambles,

Love, a desire of fools.

-Ursula Lumpkin

Sworn To Secrecy

Title: _____

At times I wonder, if you know, when you look my way, I'll do anything for you.

Instead, I choose pain, than to let you kink my armor or threaten my fragile ego.

You are immortal.

What meager men gaze at the moon and yearn for,

Chimera.

-Ursula Lumpkin

Sworn To Secrecy

Title: _____

How can it be finding someone new, when everyone I seek will have characteristics of you?

-Ursula Lumpkin

Sworn To Secrecy

Title: _____

Callous stares,

Deafening whispers,

The expectation of non-education.

The faux smiles and low stature,

The differentiation of pigmentation,

    the divide in this sovereign nation.

If I could take this color off.

Born into another's sin.

We mourn for generations.

Strength overshadowed by tears.

Black overshadowed by black.

If I could take this color off.

-Ursula Lumpkin

Sworn To Secrecy

Title: _____

When you need a break from this world, you don't mean me.

I want you to wrinkle from laughing for a lifetime.

Keep your hands in mine.

Understand, when I shed tears, it's because word like 'beautiful' won't suffice.

Let's name stars together.

-Ursula Lumpkin

Sworn To Secrecy

Title: _____

I miss you like the night will miss the moon if it never reappeared.

Here come the tears.

The urge to soothe my ego overbears the longing to hear you speak.

Do me justice, don't bury me too deep.

Think of me in crowded rooms, see me when you sleep.

Leave me to my futile sobs, the breeze will dry my cheeks.

Weeping willows, you know how I feel?

-Ursula Lumpkin

Sworn To Secrecy

Title: _____

Stars don't shine the same.

The moon seems farther.

Days are longer.

I miss you now.

Offer me always, and wherever you are, I am too.

-Ursula Lumpkin

Sworn To Secrecy

Title: _____

The pause between words is the hardest part.

Just tell me.

Cut me with every word than by hesitation.

Make me feel everything, instead of nothing.

You're still the sweetest thing.

-Ursula Lumpkin

Sworn To Secrecy

Title: _____

I'm selfish.

I'll admit.

Who are you sharing your wisdom with?

Who's been deemed your favorite?

Who can ruffle your feathers like me?

More importantly,

Who's going to love me now?

I'm selfish.

You were for me.

Do angels really sing?

Can I touch your wings?

-Ursula Lumpkin

Sworn To Secrecy

Title: _____

No one told me of the suffering,

Or how to stop the aching,

Or the remedy for regret.

Everyone has her name.

Never felt this pain?

I resent you, I've got time, hours feel like days.

Did I provoke you Venus, in my many moments of disdain?

A woman scorned, we are one, let's sustain this rage.

-Ursula Lumpkin

Sworn To Secrecy

Title: _____

What if the moon was never full?

What if it never rained purple?

What if Othello believed Desdemona?

What if waves never reached the shore?

What if the Mona Lisa was completed?

I wonder.

What if she didn't bite the apple?

What if Romeo was buried beside Juliet?

What if there were 6 wonders instead of 7?

What if Van Gogh kept his ear?

What if I never fell in love that one time?

Could I have found you sooner?

-Ursula Lumpkin

Sworn To Secrecy

Title: _____

Rivers to cross,

Streams to frolic,

Plenty of mistakes to make.

Tears to dry,

Lies to tell,

A few more hearts to break.

Stars to name,

Romps in the rain,

A kiss for old time's sake.

A hand to hold,

A vow to take,

A life, hesitant to create.

Energy transformed,

My maker to meet,

Oh, what a delightful wait.

-Ursula Lumpkin

Sworn To Secrecy

Title: _____

Is it cliché to say, I need you?

I need you to need me too.

The agony.

Your lies are so sincere, teach me to do that.

Watch my lips when I speak to you.

Behave yourself when I'm near you.

Beg for me to notice you.

I need you to need me too.

-Ursula Lumpkin

Sworn To Secrecy

Title: _____

Everything went silent.

Babies stopped crying.

The wind shifted.

I've felt truth,

She only smiled at me.

-Ursula Lumpkin

Sworn To Secrecy

Title: _____

Joy in knowing you won't be the same,

Content with letting you try.

If I were a more compassionate person, I would've wished for a longer night.

On this day, we were here, and chose loss instead.

-Ursula Lumpkin

Sworn To Secrecy

Title: _____

Meet me where dandelions sway and bougainvilleas bloom,

Where the air is dim and the rain gives you chills,

Where waterfalls flow into streams, and grass isn't always green,

Where the night is obsidian, and Sirius is the only star that gleams,

Where the moon is so full, you can watch the dolphins play,

Meet me there or stay away.

-Ursula Lumpkin

Sworn To Secrecy

Title: _____

You picked an opportune time to leave.

Just the thought makes me scream.

The sun has set, the eagles turned back,

Can stars turn black?

Please bring rain to hide my tears.

Please bring chaos to hide my fears.

My dream catcher works too well,

I prefer to see you,

Even in nightmares.

-Ursula Lumpkin

Sworn To Secrecy

Title: _____

I, being of sound mind, not acting under duress or undue influence, devise and bequeath thee:

Serenity. For putting my soul at ease, when the world was against me.

Gratitude. A times I like to tempt fate, by denying me, you saved me.

Peace. All your lies must cause you grief.

Darkness. Without it, how can there be light?

I offer these in abundance.

-Ursula Lumpkin

Sworn To Secrecy

Thank you for supporting. I hope you enjoy reading this book as much as I enjoyed writing it. My wish is that something I wrote touched you and made you comfortable in feeling emotions that you would normally not share with anyone. You are not alone, feel everything, show emotion, it's ok to do so. Thank you to the ones that are silently clapping for me, and to the ones that have watched me grow. Thank you to the ones that give me nuggets of wisdom when I feel lost. Thank you to the community where I was raised, it really takes a village. Thank you to the friends and loved ones that have come and gone, each one teaching me something. I'd like to thank myself for having the courage to put this book out into the universe.

Thank you. Thank you. Thank you.

Truly yours,

Ursula Lumpkin

Sworn To Secrecy

www.ingramcontent.com/pod-product-compliance
Lightning Source LLC
Chambersburg PA
CBHW021358300426
44114CB00012B/1278